Whiskey
and the
Autumn Wind

By Richard White

A Collection of Poems in Hemingway Tradition

Dedication

To my father, John White,

Your strength and unwavering hope, even in the face of your own mistakes, have always inspired me to dream big and persevere. You were stubborn and steadfast, never giving up, and I often wonder if you are proud of me.

In memory of you, as we release this book on your birthday, December 31st, I honor the legacy you left behind.

Your spirit lives on in these words, as they dance through the autumn wind.

With all my love, your son

Richard

Acknowledgements

This book was inspired by Kenny Chesney's song "Hemingway's Whiskey," which resonated deeply with me and fueled my creative journey. The song's evocative storytelling and emotional depth served as a catalyst for my exploration of themes that blend the timeless allure of traditional poetry with contemporary reflections.

I would also like to express my heartfelt gratitude for my enduring love of traditional poetry, which has shaped my writing and continues to inspire me every day. Thank you to all the poets and writers whose works have guided me on this literary path.

Table of Contents

The Autumn's Final Breath
The Scent of Leaves and Amber
The Taste of Autumn's Flame
The Whiskey's Breath in Autumn's hand
The Leaves Speak in Whiskey's Tone
The Whiskey's Gentle Embrace
The Autumn's Love, The Whiskey's Glow
The Bourbon's Promise in the Wind
A Love Found in Autumn's Flame
The Ember's Whisper
Harvest of the Heart
The Wistful Wind
Echoes of the Hearth
Autumn's Embrace
Aged in Autumn
The Fireside Reverie
Maple's Whisper
Autumn Glass
Smoke and Firelight
Ember and Ash
The Amber Hours
Honeyed Fire
Autumn's Gold
The Autumn Remembers
Echo of Her Eyes
The Fire That Won't Fade
The Woman in the Glass
A Quiet Burning
In the Absence of Sound
A Memory Distilled
Autumn's Alchemy
The Glass That Holds Her Memory
The Alchemy of Loss
The Heart's Burden

The Spirit's Folly
Autumn's Pour
At Dusk, By the Fire
In the Quiet
Old Oak and Fire
A Toast to the Night
In Autumn's Shadow
Where Fire and the Shadow Meet
Under the Autumn Moon
The Familiar Sting
The Last Watch
Autumn's Quiet Burden
A Solitary Toast
The Glass and Autumn's Fire
Leaves Fall with a Soldier's Burden
Unnamed
Ashes on the Breeze
The Amber Flame
The Soldier's Autumn
Autumn Wind
Whiskey's Breath
Autumn Whiskey
The River's Quiet Grace
The Last Cigarette
Whiskey and Autumn Winds
A Slow Burn in the Autumn Light
Bourbon's Confession
Amber Harvest
A Pantoum of Maple and Fire
Melancholy of the Flame
The Forest Speaks in Amber Hues
Cinamon Winds
A Pantoum of Hearth and Smoke
Maple's Melancholy

Preface

In the ever-changing seasons of life, we often find ourselves seeking solace and understanding in the familiar embrace of nature and the warmth of cherished memories. This collection of poetry, "Whiskey and the Autumn Wind," is a testament to those moments of introspection, where the gentle rustle of leaves and the rich, amber glow of whiskey offer a refuge from the tumult of our inner struggles.

Inspired by the evocative storytelling of Kenny Chesney's song "Hemingway's Whiskey," this book delves into the depths of human emotion, blending the timeless allure of traditional poetry with contemporary reflections. The song's narrative resonated deeply within me, igniting a creative spark that guided my exploration of themes such as fire and warmth, isolation and introspection, harvest and abundance, nostalgia and reflection, and the comforting embrace of nature's hues.

As I penned these verses, I found myself repeatedly drawn to the image of an older man, seated by a crackling fireplace, savoring a glass of whiskey while lost in thought. This figure, much like the essence of this book, embodies the juxtaposition of inner darkness and light, the dance of shadows and warmth, and the relentless pursuit of understanding and peace.

This collection is dedicated to my father, John White, whose strength and unwavering hope, even in the face of his own mistakes, have always inspired me to dream big and persevere. His stubborn and steadfast nature, never giving up despite the odds, has been a guiding force in my life. As we release this book on his birthday, December 31st , I honor the legacy he left behind. I often wonder if he is proud of me, and I hope that these words, carried by the autumn wind, reach him wherever he may be.

To my father, your spirit lives on in these pages. To Kenny Chesney, whose song sparked this journey, and to all the poets and writers who have illuminated my path, I offer my deepest gratitude.

May these poems provide you, dear reader, with a sense of comfort, introspection, and connection, as they have for me.

Roots and Rivers

Whiskey slides smooth, like a river at dusk,
Over tongue and teeth, warming the bones.
Earth settles on the taste, rich as dark soil,
Reminds me of forests, the smell of rain,
Leaves falling without a sound.

In this amber moment, I think of life —
How it moves, rough, then soft, then still.
Like the whiskey, it burns, then soothes,
Leaves its mark, quiet as the wind
Whispering through pine.

The glass, half-full, half-empty —
Same as every season,
Same as every man,
Rooted deep in the ground
But always reaching toward the sky.

Traces of the Earth

Whiskey flows, a golden stream,
Its warmth a quiet, whispered dream,
With earthy tones that linger long,
Like moss and soil, rich and strong.

It rests upon my tongue like rain
That falls on fields of autumn grain,
And in its taste, the wild appears,
Of distant woods and passing years.

I sip and think of nature's way,
Of dawn and dusk, of night and day,
How life, like whiskey, smooth and slow,
Leaves traces of the earth below.

Mirror of Paths

Whiskey pours, a silent thread,
A nod to life, a glance at death.
The glass reflects both night and dawn,
A flicker here, soon to be gone.

Its earthy taste, like roots in clay,
Clings to the tongue, then slips away —
A mirror of the paths we tread,
Where every breath is something shed.

We live, we laugh, we curse the flame,
Yet in the end, we're much the same.
Like whiskey's burn, we flare, then fade,
Returning to the earth we made.

The irony, in glass or tomb —
We're born, we rise, and face the gloom.
Still, whiskey smooth, or bitter fight,
Both end beneath the stars' cold light.

Toast to Life

The whiskey swirls, a fading light,
In shadows deep, just out of sight.
Each sip, a step toward unseen ground,
Where silence waits, without a sound.

The earth it holds, a whisper clear,
Like autumn leaves, the end draws near.
I taste the forest, damp and still,
The weight of time, the coming chill.

There's something in the amber hue,
A warning soft, yet sharp and true —
Like Persephone, drawn below,
We drink, we dance, then let it go.

For in this glass, I see the night,
The final dark, the fading light.
A toast to life, a nod to death,
Before we draw our last, deep breath.

A Toast to Dusk

Maple bourbon swirls, a quiet flame,
In amber depths, it knows the name.
Each sip, a step toward fading dusk,
Where time slips by in shadows' husk.

The earth is sweet, with maple's kiss,
Yet in the taste, there lies abyss.
I feel the woods, the autumn air,
A hint of frost, a chill laid bare.

There's something in this bourbon's glow,
A whisper soft, a truth we know —
Like autumn leaves, bound to fall,
We drink, we laugh, then heed the call.

For in this glass, I taste the end,
Where life's last threads begin to bend.
A toast to days, a nod to night,
Before we vanish from the light.

Fire Within

On a bitter chill, when winter's breath
Wraps the world in icy death,
Maple bourbon warms the glass,
A golden light as shadows pass.

I lift the cup, its warmth within,
A comfort found, a fleeting grin.
The fire crackles, embers glow,
While outside howls the wind and snow.

Each sip, a balm for frostbitten days,
Like sunbeams breaking through the haze.
The sweet embrace of maple's touch,
A gentle hug, it means so much.

As the cold bites through every seam,
This warming drink ignites a dream —
Of summer fields, of flowers bright,
Of life returning, pure delight.

So let the world outside be cold,
For in my heart, a fire holds.
With maple bourbon, I'll brave the chill,
And toast to warmth, my spirit's will.

The Amber Gaze

In shadows deep, I sit alone,
A glass of amber by me shown.
The whiskey's warmth, a fleeting balm,
Yet in my heart, I find no calm.

Each sip, a whisper of the past,
Of dreams once bright, now shadows cast.
Within this glow, I seek the light,
But find instead the endless night.

The Thirst of Madness

The bourbon swirls, a tempest bold,
In every drop, my fears unfold.
This amber drink, it masks the pain,
Yet deep inside, I fear the strain.

The world outside, a distant song,
Where reason fades, and I feel wrong.
A mind unraveled, a heart laid bare,
In whiskey's glow, I breathe despair.

The Hiding Place

I hide within this glassy sphere,
Where all my thoughts can disappear.
The whiskey's fire, a false embrace,
It warms my soul but leaves no trace.

Lost in the depths of amber hue,
A prison forged of dreams untrue.
Yet here I linger, lost in time,
A captive heart, a silent crime.

The Echo of Solitude

The winter's chill surrounds my frame,
As bourbon calls me by its name.
In liquid gold, my troubles fade,
But in the depths, my mind is frayed.

Each drop consumed, a step away,
From reason's grasp, from light of day.
In whiskey's dance, I seek to flee,
Yet find my heart in endless sea.

The Lament of the Lost

In flickering light, the shadows creep,
As I sip from this glass, my secrets keep.
The bourbon's warmth, a sweet disguise,
Yet madness stirs beneath my sighs.

Each amber drop, a fleeting balm,
To quiet the storm and grant me calm.
But deep within, a tempest churns,
For hope once bright now slowly burns.

Oh, the world outside, a distant dream,
Where laughter rings and spirits gleam.
Yet here I dwell, in solitude's hold,
A wanderer lost, with heart turned cold.

The whispers echo, the silence grows,
In bourbon's glow, my sorrow flows.
Though time may pass, and shadows wane,
I linger still, in this aching pain.

The Bitter Draught

The rum, it pours with heavy hand,
A tide that sweeps away the sand.
In each dark drop, I seek reprieve,
From thoughts of you I can't unweave.

The taste is sweet, yet sorrow hides,
Behind its warmth, where silence bides.
I drink, and in the amber gloom,
The echoes of your name consume.

Oh, I once held you close and near,
But now the rum must drown the tear.
For every sip, a shadow cast,
Of love that faded far too fast.

Still, in the glow, a future lies —
A void, where all our mem'ries die.
Yet as the glass drains in the night,
I feel the pull of endless night.

Though rum may steal your face away,
I know, within, you'll always stay.
For in this draught, the dark forewarns,
That even lost, my soul still mourns.

The Autumn's Whisper

The trees, they whisper, clothed in flame,
Their leaves of gold call out my name.
In every branch, a story told,
Of fleeting youth, and growing old.

The orange skies, the dying sun,
A mirror to the race we run.
Each yellow leaf, a page unfurled,
Of autumn's book, an aging world.

The whiskey in my hand does speak,
Its amber glow both soft and bleak.
It murmurs low of time now passed,
And days too sweet to ever last.

The red leaves dance like fleeting fire,
A final blaze of lost desire.
They fall as I take one last sip,
As nature's hues and whiskey slip —

Together they foretell the end,
A world that bends, yet won't defend.
And in this autumn's fleeting light,
The amber warns of endless night.

The Whiskey Wind

The wind in autumn takes its turn,
With every gust, the leaves do burn.
"Come," it whispers to the trees,
"Let go, give in, to me, release."

The whiskey laughs, it knows the way,
How all things fade, how none can stay.
It clinks against the crystal rim,
A song of fate, both full and grim.

The reds and golds, the amber fire,
Of whiskey and the leaves' desire,
Entwine with wind, a dance of death,
As nature draws her final breath.

And as I watch the autumn fall,
The whiskey tells me, after all,
That even wind, so wild and free,
Will someday still, as all must be.

So sip the amber, feel the breeze,
And watch the dying of the trees.
For in their hues, the truth is told —
That all things fade, and all grow cold.

Whiskey and the Autumn Wind

The autumn wind, with sighs so deep,
Does through the barren branches creep.
It stirs the leaves, in gold and red,
A final dance for all things dead.

I sit and watch with glass in hand,
The whiskey's glow like embered sand.
It warms my lips, my spirit's core,
Yet still, I crave the peace once more.

The wind, it howls as twilight falls,
And whispers through the forest halls.
It speaks of days, long gone from sight,
Of youth now lost, and fading light.

Each sip I take, the earth grows still,
As whiskey bends the world to will.
The amber burns, then smooths away,
Like life itself, both night and day.

So let the wind and whiskey blend,
For both shall meet where all things end.
The autumn's breath, the amber's glow,
Both whisper truths we always know.

The Fireside's Flicker

The fire burns with steady flame,
Its warmth, a friend I cannot name.
It holds the chill of night at bay,
Yet cannot keep the years away.

I sit alone, the hearth aglow,
The whiskey's heat, so soft and slow.
It whispers tales of harvest days,
When time was ripe, in golden haze.

But now I drink and sit in thought,
Of all the warmth that I once sought.
Though fire flickers, bright and true,
It warms the air, but not what's due.

For irony in flames does lie —
That even warmth must one day die.

The Harvest's Spoils

The fields were full in autumn's hand,
We reaped the riches of the land.
The grain was gold, the days were long,
Each moment passed like simple song.

Yet here I sit with cup in hand,
The fruit of toil, the whiskey grand.
I drink to all those days of light,
And wonder where they went, so slight.

For harvest comes and harvest goes,
It gives, then leaves us with what grows —
Not fruit, not grain, but thoughts that swell,
Of days now lost, we know too well.

In abundance, there is despair —
For nothing lasts, no field, no care.

The Hearth's Embrace

The hearth does glow, a steady friend,
Its fire's warmth shall never bend.
With bourbon's burn upon my tongue,
The autumn wind outside has sung.

The glass sits full, the amber gleams,
A comfort found in fading dreams.
The taste, it lingers soft yet bold,
A hint of warmth as nights grow cold.

Yet in this heat, a truth must speak—
For even fires fade to weak.
The glow may soothe, the drink may heal,
But all is fleeting, none is real.

The autumn wind, it knocks once more,
A chill that even bourbon can't restore.

The Aftertaste of Years

I sip the bourbon, rich and pure,
Its warmth, a balm I can't ignore.
Yet on the tongue, the aftertaste,
Reminds me of the time I've chased.

The harvest's done, the fields are bare,
The wind is crisp with biting air.
But in the glass, a world remains,
Of summers lost, and autumn's gains.

The warmth it brings, it dulls the chill,
But deeper still, the heart grows still.
For all this comfort, all this heat,
Can't chase away the cold defeat.

In autumn's wind, the taste lingers long,
A fleeting warmth before it's gone.

The Autumn's Breath

The autumn wind breathes through the trees,
It whispers low in gentle pleas.
The bourbon swirls, a golden thread,
While leaves like embers fall, now dead.

I drink, and with each passing draught,
The warmth and wind play soft and daft.
The fire cracks, a hollow song,
A fleeting comfort, brief, yet strong.

But winds will blow, and fires fade,
No warmth can halt what's been delayed.
For time moves on, as wind does howl,
And whiskey's glow cannot endow.

The amber hue may fill my glass,
Yet in its depths, all things must pass.

The Lasting Flame

The fire flickers, steadfast, true,
It casts its glow in amber hue.
The bourbon's heat is bold and bright,
A fleeting warmth in autumn's night.

The taste, it dances on the tongue,
A song unsung, a bell once rung.
But in its fire, there lies a chill,
A quiet truth, unmoved, yet still.

For as I drink, the world unwinds,
The fire dims, the night reminds—
That even warmth, so deeply sought,
Is but a brief, forgotten thought.

The autumn's wind may carry far,
Yet none can hold its fading star.

The Bourbon's Kiss

She moves like bourbon in the glass,
A golden glow, so smooth to pass.
Her warmth, it lingers on my lips,
Like amber flames in gentle sips.

Her breath, a breeze in autumn's night,
Her touch, the fire's tender light.
She burns with heat, yet soft as silk,
Like bourbon rich, as sweet as milk.

And as I drink, I feel her near,
Her warmth dispels the autumn's fear.
Yet whiskey, like her fleeting grace,
Leaves only echoes in its place.

For both will warm, then both will fade,
A love, like bourbon, slowly made.

In Her Whiskey Eyes

Her eyes, like whiskey, dark and deep,
Hold secrets that the nights must keep.
With every glance, they burn so bright,
A fire within the autumn's night.

She flows like bourbon in my veins,
A warmth that soothes, then softly wanes.
The taste of her, a heady blend,
That pulls me close, yet knows no end.

But like the whiskey's gentle burn,
She too will leave, and not return.
For in her heat, a cold resides,
A truth that neither love nor hides.

And as the wind howls through the trees,
I sip her name in autumn's breeze.

The Pine's Secret

Beneath the pines, the wind does speak,
Of secrets old, and whispers weak.
The maple whiskey fills the air,
Its sweetness touched by something rare.

The taste of earth, a forest deep,
Where shadows in the needles creep.
The amber hue, a fleeting sight,
Like moonlit paths in autumn's night.

Yet in its sweetness, there's a trace,
Of something darker, lost in space.
The pine trees bend, their breath so still,
As whiskey flows to match their will.

For in this drink, a truth does lie—
The sweetness fades, and all must die.

The Amber Grove

The whiskey smells of maple trees,
Of autumn's heart and autumn's breeze.
Yet in its taste, there lies a shade,
A promise, and a price now paid.

The pines, they watch with needles keen,
And in their bark, the years have seen.
Each drop of amber, rich and sweet,
Tells tales of lives, both brief and fleet.

For in the whiskey's burn I find,
A forest lost, a hidden mind.
Its taste is warm, but underneath,
The scent of pine foretells the wreath.

And as I sip, the night grows near,
The wind, it whispers, soft with fear.

The Whiskey's Veil

The night does fall, a velvet shroud,
The maple whiskey speaks aloud.
Its burn is gentle, yet it sings,
Of autumn leaves and secret things.

The pine trees sway, their boughs so wide,
They hide the stars the moon won't guide.
Within their scent, a shadow lies,
A warning in the amber skies.

Each sip reveals a darker truth,
Of fleeting days, and stolen youth.
The fire warms, but whispers low,
That all things bright must cease to glow.

And though the whiskey soothes my fears,
It cannot turn the tide of years.

Beneath the Harvest Moon

Beneath the harvest moon's pale gleam,
I drink to those who chase a dream.
The whiskey's taste, so rich and clear,
A fleeting warmth, a fading cheer.

The maple's sweetness coats the air,
A hint of fire, a lover's snare.
Yet in its depths, a silence grows,
Like whispers in the pine that blows.

For autumn's wind, though soft and bright,
Will steal away the longest night.
The fire flickers, bourbon's kiss,
Reminds me of what once was bliss.

But as the leaves begin to fall,
I see the end within it all.

The Amber's Song

The whiskey hums a quiet tune,
Beneath the sky, the amber moon.
Its taste, like flame, both sharp and sweet,
A lover's touch, both sure and fleet.

The pine trees bend to hear its sound,
A mournful song that knows no bound.
The wind it carries all that's past,
A gentle breath that cannot last.

I sip the bourbon, rich and bold,
Its warmth, a shield against the cold.
Yet in its depths, I taste the end,
A journey winding to descend.

For even sweetness hides the night,
Where shadows take the final light.

The Autumn's Final Breath

The autumn wind, so soft, so still,
Has whispered long, and bends its will.
The whiskey swirls within my glass,
A mirror to the days that pass.

Its amber hue, a fleeting fire,
Like love once felt, like old desire.
I taste the pine, the earth, the wood,
A truth not known, but understood.

For in this drink, a fate does dwell,
A quiet tale, a solemn bell.
The sweetness fades, the warmth is gone,
And autumn takes her final dawn.

Yet as the wind begins to wane,
The whiskey whispers once again.

The Scent of Leaves and Amber

The autumn leaves, they crack and fall,
Their scent a call, a whispered thrall.
The whiskey swirls, its breath like fire,
A taste of smoke, a slow desire.

The maple scent does fill the air,
Like forests bending in a prayer.
Each leaf, like bourbon, sweet and warm,
Now dances in the autumn's storm.

The trees, they speak in amber tones,
Their branches creak like tired bones.
And whiskey, too, in golden streams,
Now flows with tales of buried dreams.

The wind, it pulls the scent away,
Yet in the glass, the fall will stay.

The Taste of Autumn's Flame

The whiskey burns, a gentle sigh,
Like autumn winds that pass us by.
It tastes of earth, of pine and bark,
Of fading days, and skies gone dark.

The maple lingers on my lips,
A touch of fire in fleeting sips.
The air is thick with leaves that fall,
Their scent, a soft, nostalgic call.

The trees, they hum in whispered tones,
Their bark, a song of time and stones.
And as I drink, the forest speaks,
Of years long past, of life's mystique.

For in each sip, the season shows,
That even flames must end their glow.

The Whiskey's Breath in Autumn's hand

The whiskey breathes in autumn's hand,
A smoky kiss across the land.
Its taste is rich with harvest's gold,
A fire warmed, but never cold.

The trees, they wear their autumn best,
In fiery hues they've long possessed.
The wind, it carries maple sweet,
And at my lips, the tastes do meet.

The leaves, they fall with whispered grace,
Their scent, like whiskey, fills the space.
Each sip, like bark beneath my tongue,
A song of days when I was young.

The bourbon laughs, a warming breath,
Yet hides the chill of winter's death.

The Leaves Speak in Whiskey's Tone

The leaves, they speak in whiskey's tone,
Their amber hues, a warmth well-known.
The scent of maple fills the breeze,
A note of fire among the trees.

Each sip, like autumn's final breath,
Now foreshadows the season's death.
The taste of oak, of pine and flame,
Echoes the world that's not the same.

The trees, they bow, their colors bright,
Yet soon will fall into the night.
The whiskey's warmth, it holds me near,
But autumn's scent is ever clear.

For in the leaves, the forest knows,
That every warmth must meet its close.

The Whiskey's Gentle Embrace

The whiskey whispers soft and low,
Its warmth a place I come to know.
Like autumn's breath upon my cheek,
It comforts me when words grow weak.

The leaves, they fall with tender grace,
A soft goodbye, an amber trace.
Their scent, like bourbon on the air,
Invites me in, beyond despair.

I taste the trust within the glass,
A quiet love that comes to pass.
The oak, the smoke, the maple's kiss,
They hold me close in tender bliss.

For in this warmth, I find my rest,
And autumn cradles me, its guest.

The Autumn's Love, The Whiskey's Glow

The trees, they sigh in autumn's glow,
Their love, like whiskey, pure and slow.
The air is sweet with maple's song,
A warmth that's felt, though time is long.

I hold the glass, its amber gleam,
A love that lingers in a dream.
The leaves, they fall like whispers true,
Reminding me of trust anew.

Each sip, a moment held in place,
A quiet smile, a lover's grace.
The whiskey's fire, soft yet strong,
It soothes the heart that's waited long.

For in this season's calm embrace,
I find the warmth, the trust, the space.

The Bourbon's Promise in the Wind

The autumn wind, it sings a tune,
As bourbon fills the early moon.
Its taste is rich with love's old vow,
A warmth that lingers even now.

The leaves, they dance in soft retreat,
Their colors fall at autumn's feet.
And in the glass, the fire's glow,
Reflects the trust I've come to know.

The whiskey's burn, a lover's care,
It wraps me in the evening air.
I feel the peace, the sweet release,
Of all that's held, now set at ease.

For autumn's hand, and bourbon's kiss,
Remind me that I live in bliss.

A Love Found in Autumn's Flame

The whiskey flows, a golden stream,
Its warmth like love, a fleeting dream.
The autumn trees, they bend and sway,
Their leaves, like vows, now fall away.

Each sip, a promise, bold and clear,
Of all that's trusted, all that's dear.
The maple's taste, a tender touch,
A love that lingers long as such.

The wind, it wraps me in its fold,
A comfort found when nights grow cold.
The fire burns, the bourbon's heat,
A love that feels both strong and sweet.

For in this autumn's fleeting grace,
I find the trust in every taste.

The Ember's Whisper

In the heart of autumn's fiery breath,
Where leaves like whispers fall to rest,
An amber glow from hearth's embrace,
Reflects the warmth of whiskey's grace.

The scent of pine and maple's sweet,
Entwine with bourbon, calm, discreet.
A tale of love, a hint of loss,
In shadows cast, where dreams emboss.

The wind, it sighs with memories old,
A dance of warmth amidst the cold.
Each sip a journey, smooth and deep,
Where secrets of the past do sleep.

Harvest of the Heart

Among the fields of autumn gold,
Where stories of the earth unfold,
A man with whiskey in his hand,
Finds solace in this quiet land.
The fire crackles, whispers low,
Of harvest moons and past's shadow.

A taste of cinnamon and spice,
Brings comfort to this paradise.
His thoughts a blend of joy and pain,
As leaves descend like gentle rain.
The bourbon's burn, a lover's touch,
In autumn's arms, he feels so much.

The Wistful Wind

Beneath the sky of twilight's hue,
Where reds and yellows paint the view,
A spirit stirs within the glass,
Reflecting on what's come to pass.

The whiskey swirls with tales untold,
Of lovers lost and hearts grown cold.
A fleeting scent of oak and smoke,
Awakens dreams with every stroke.

In solitude, the man does find,
A peace within the autumn wind.
The past and present intertwine,
In amber's glow, a fate divine.

Echoes of the Hearth

By the hearth, where flames do dance,
He sits alone in a silent trance.
The warmth of bourbon on his tongue,
Recalls a time when he was young.

The leaves outside in colors bright,
Mirror the fire's flickering light.
A hint of sorrow, sweet and low,
In whiskey's depths, emotions flow.

The harvest yields both joy and woe,
As autumn's whispers gently blow.
In every sip, a story dwells,
Of love and loss, where memory swells.

Autumn's Embrace

In the chill of autumn's twilight,
Where shadows lengthen,
and day takes flight,
An old man finds his solace there,
With whiskey's warmth and autumn air.

The scent of leaves and woodsmoke blend,
With memories that never end.
A sip of maple whiskey sweet,
Brings echoes of the past's heartbeat.

The wind's soft murmur through the trees,
Carries whispers on the breeze.
In fire's glow, his heart does rest,
Embraced by autumn, wholly blessed.

Aged in Autumn

The years have passed like falling leaves,
Yet in his heart, he still believes,
That love, like bourbon aged and rare,
Can warm the soul and ease despair.

The fire's glow, a steady light,
Against the coming of the night.
In amber liquid, he does find,
A peace that soothes his troubled mind.

The autumn wind, a gentle kiss,
Reminds him of forgotten bliss.
Each sip a journey through the years,
A blend of laughter, hopes, and tears.

The Fireside Reverie

By the fireside,
where warmth abides,
He lets the whiskey be his guide.
The autumn leaves outside do fall,
A silent witness to it all.

The scent of cinnamon,
rich and bold,
Weaves stories from the days of old.
In each sip, a life retold,
Of love once warm,
now grown cold.

Yet in this solitude,
he finds,
A comfort in the autumn winds.
The whiskey's burn,
a gentle touch,
In memories,
he finds so much.

Maple's Whisper

In the quiet of the autumn night,
With stars above and firelight,
 He lifts his glass of maple gold,
And lets the evening's tale unfold.

The taste of whiskey,
smooth and sweet,
A solace in this calm retreat.
The leaves outside,
a rustling choir,
Sing softly of a love's desire.

The autumn wind,
with gentle grace,
Caresses him in its embrace.
In every sip, a whisper lies,
Of bygone days and tender sighs.

Autumn Glass

I watch the fire dance, whiskey in hand,
Its amber glow, warm against the glass —
Hints of oak, of time gone slow and wise,
Aged like the burn of autumn on the trees.

The cigar, smoldering like dusk,
Draws a line between thought and silence.
Outside, the wind stirs leaves on brittle ground,
Rustling secrets only October knows.

Each sip heavy, seasoned, sure —
The taste of endings and things that stay.
And in the stillness, I feel it settle:
The comfort of fire, a smoke-laden sky,
The quiet weight of lives I have lived,
And the truth of this one, here in my hands.

Smoke and Firelight

Whiskey rests in the glass like old regrets,
And the fire crackles low, in tune with the night.
Smoke curls from the cigar, hangs in the air,
As if waiting for words too heavy to say.

I lean back and let autumn breathe through the
window, Let it wrap around like an old coat,
The smell of wood, of leaves letting go,
Of cold on the edge of firelight's reach.

It's a moment suspended — quiet and worn,
Nothing chasing, nothing to win.
Just the warmth of the burn, the hiss of a log,
And the long, low ache of knowing what's gone.

Ember and Ash

The whiskey pools slow, gold as dying light,
Warming my hand as the evening wanes.
Each sip tastes of memory — smoke and spice,
And autumn's breath, crisp and close.

Outside, the world turns bronze and gray,
Leaves drift down like the remnants of years,
Falling and falling, gone before they're grasped,
Just a season passing through the glass.

The cigar dims, a smolder to match the fire,
Ash falling soft as a whispered name.
I take a breath, draw the smoke deep,
Feel it settle where words no longer reach.

In the glow of the hearth, time feels frayed,
Each moment unspooling, each silence a thread,
And there's comfort here, in whiskey's weight,
In the warmth of things I'll let drift away.

The Amber Hours

It's whiskey and dusk, and the hours grow thick,
The fire soft against the deepening night.
There's a quiet there, rich as aged wood,
A stillness shaped by autumn's hand.

I hold the glass like an old friend's grip,
Solid and sure, a memory kept close.
Hints of maple, of pine, of something wild,
A taste of the earth, rough and unrefined.

Outside, the leaves sweep past the window,
Burnished gold, like secrets let go.
They fall, one by one, in shadows and light,
And somewhere in their descent, I feel it too —
The letting go, the calm release,
In the slow amber burn of whiskey's peace.

Honeyed Fire

A cool wind stirs the amber leaves,
As day descends, as light deceives.
In twilight's blush, the colors blaze,
Like embers caught in autumn's haze.

The honeyed whiskey warms my lips,
Its sweetness slow, its fire drips
Down steady, deep, a golden tide,
To spark a flame I hold inside.

The fire crackles, soft and low,
A tune the trees and breezes know.
Around me, colors rich and bright,
Reflect the warmth of fading light.

In smoke and scent, in taste and hue,
I find the world both old and new.
The fire, the leaves, the whiskey's gleam —
A fleeting breath, a living dream.

Autumn's Gold

Honey whiskey, smooth and sweet,
A fire's glow, the day's retreat.
Afternoon fades, cool and fair,
As gold and crimson paint the air.

Leaves drift softly to the ground,
In whirls of color, all unbound.
They dance as if the season's close
Brought every tree a fiery prose.

Each sip brings warmth, each taste a spark,
As autumn settles, crisp and stark.
The honey lingers, soft and pure,
A fleeting sweetness to endure.

With firelight's glow, I sit and see
The world in autumn's majesty —
In whiskey's warmth, in colors deep,
A moment's solace mine to keep.

The Autumn Remembers

The whiskey swirls, amber and deep,
As leaves drift down in piles to sleep.
I drink to lose her face, her voice,
To silence youth's relentless choice.

Yet here in autumn's gentle hold,
I see her hair, dark as the fold
Of midnight's quiet, wild and free —
A memory whiskey can't quite flee.

Her eyes, brown as chestnut's shine,
Glimpse back at me through oak and pine.
They haunt the glass, the burn and taste,
In memories neither slow nor chased.

And though I drink to let her fade,
This amber fire has her remade —
She lingers, caught in autumn's breath,
A beauty sharp as summer's death.

Echo of Her Eyes

Each sip, a warmth, a fading light,
In autumn's chill, in evening's bite.
The whiskey holds a hollow heat,
A comfort bound in calm defeat.

Her dark hair falls like autumn's shade,
Her laughter lost in paths we made.
I drink, I try to turn away,
Yet see her there as leaves decay.

Those eyes, dark brown, a smoldered hue,
Peer back from shadows, deep and true.
Though time and taste may blur her face,
In whiskey's burn, I find her trace.

Each drop I raise in dim regret
Awakens love I'd best forget—
Yet there she is, like autumn's flame,
A spark alive within my shame.

The Fire That Won't Fade

She was half my years, a passing dream,
Dark-eyed, like secrets left unseen.
I drink to lose her, sip by sip,
But there she stirs upon my lips.

Her hair, like nightfall's soft embrace,
Dark as the shadows time can't chase.
And though I wish her far away,
In whiskey's warmth, her memory stays.

Beneath the maples' russet leaves,
Her laughter haunts the autumn eves.
The drink may dull, yet can't erase
Her ghostly form in autumn's grace.

So here I sit, mid-age and worn,
With whiskey's taste, both sweet and torn—
To drown her face, her youth, her eyes,
Yet find her there as each leaf dies.

The Woman in the Glass

She lingers here, a fleeting trace,
A woman young, a long-lost face.
Her dark hair like the autumn night,
Her brown eyes warm, a lover's light.

The whiskey numbs, yet wakes the fire,
A taste that fuels both love and ire.
Her memory, faint as leaves on wind,
Returns each sip, though time has thinned.

Her laughter echoes, soft and near,
In shadows cast, in fires clear.
Though half my years, she fills the glass —
A haunting I can't help but pass.

So here I drink, alone and still,
With whiskey's burn, both sharp and chill.
I try to drown her, year by year,
Yet find her face, forever near.

A Quiet Burning

Amber in glass, a distilled silence,
a warmth held hostage in the shape of fire,
both sharp and soft, a paradox —
liquid smoke, yet clear as memory.
It rests upon the tongue, heavy as history,
a tempered heat, the color of old wounds,
of leaves caught in the red of their fall.

Autumn peers in, with her ochre eyes,
windswept, hushed — a lover unseen yet close.
She haunts the edges of the glass,
a specter in rust and bone and flame.
The taste curls, low and earthy, beneath
the language of oak, under bark-dark skies,
whiskey like a whisper of wildwood.

This is no forgetting, no retreat;
it's surrender by slow degrees,
a quiet burning to kindle the chill,
to bind the body against all fading.
What irony, that this should linger
like embers at the edge of dusk —
a heat as fleeting as the year itself.

In the Absence of Sound

Cinnamon and smoke, sharp on the air,
a fracture of light in a dark-hued hour,
as whiskey gathers, amber and dense,
in a silence shaped by waiting.

It flows with the weight of the oak it bore,
a cask's embrace, rich and resolute,
each drop a graveyard of autumn's blaze,
fallen in glory, in sacrifice to this.

Outside, the earth takes on its own burn,
gold to rust to ashen brown,
leaves scattered like forgotten words,
a contradiction of beauty in decay.
This whiskey, too, fades into warmth,
an irony — sweetness coaxed from time.

I sip, and the taste holds, deep and bitter;
each note hums of endings without grief,
a patience built on knowing when to fall,
how to linger, how to leave nothing behind.

A Memory Distilled

In the glass lies the memory of fire,
captured and kept in liquid amber,
a leaf's last gasp, a forest's echo,
autumn in repose, though it slips from my grasp.

Its scent rises in rings of wood and spice,
hemlock's shadow, the tremor of cedar —
a drink both rooted and restless,
its heat whispers against the chill.

Outside, autumn settles its debts;
the trees let go without resistance.
Leaves, coppered and brown, yield to earth,
the season folding into itself in layers.

Irony lives in the whiskey's burn,
warmth found where there is only loss,
a comfort built of sharpness and decay,
of sweetness lost upon the tongue,
left like a lover who lives in memory —
here, then gone, then here again.

Autumn's Alchemy

This glass—no more than autumn's relic,
a distillation of sun and soil and age.
The whiskey speaks, wordlessly, of flame,
of nights tempered by the edge of frost.

Each sip draws from leaves long fallen,
the burn of time, of iron and smoke,
its taste of solitude pressed from silence,
a warmth set deep as marrow's ache.

Outside, the landscape takes its cue,
a tapestry of rust and withered gold,
falling quietly as though by design,
a process too patient to bear witness.

And here I am, partaking in this alchemy,
imbibing endings, tasting quiet deaths.
To drink is to forget the cold,
a moment's irony, a comfort earned—
while autumn herself fades beyond the glass,
left to simmer in fire's last breath.

The Glass That Holds Her Memory

This glass I hold, a silent curse,
etched in amber, steeped in verse,
and through its depth, your face I see,
a specter bound in rye's decree.
Each sip, a touch of burning grace,
yet sweeter still for holding place —
the ghost of you, in fire's embrace.

I'd drain the world to drown your name,
to quench this ever-burning flame.
Moonlight's gaze and midnight's cheer,
but still you linger, crystal-clear.
What irony, this vessel's bond,
for though I drink, you linger on.

The Alchemy of Loss

Beneath the stars, in autumn's guise,
I drink the moon's reflected lies;
a bottle's hold, a lover's snare,
yet no relief is waiting there.
In fire's bite and wood's bold stain,
I sought escape, but found more pain —
for each deep draught returns again.

Whiskey's warmth, a fleeting balm,
yet stirs no peace, and brings no calm.
Through ancient oak and amber's hue,
I find the ache, still bound to you.
The world's finest spirits may vie to console,
yet none shall ransom this haunted soul.

The Heart's Burden

Oh cruel and bitter flame of rye,
you burn yet leave me dry.
How oft I thought your flames would rend
the memory that would never end.
Each glass, a prayer for peaceful night,
a balm against love's fateful blight.
Yet, in my veins, you carve her trace —
the ghostly form, her shadowed face.

O whiskey, grant me now reprieve,
though fleeting, let me scarce believe
her eyes are not in every pour,
her voice, a murmur from before.
To drink is thus to mourn anew,
for none can free me, none but you.

The Spirit's Folly

I've called upon the finest flame,
Woodford rye to curse her name;
a draught of fire, yet cold as death,
this whiskey holds her haunted breath.
The hearth's bright crackle warms my hand,
but chills my soul, a barren land.
She lingers there, within the fire,
in every taste and each desire.

The earth is rich, the leaves decay,
the autumn's hand sweeps life away;
yet, bound within this crystal glass,
her face endures, though seasons pass.
So here I sit, alone to pine,
for whiskey brings no peace of mind.

Autumn's Pour

Amber light slants through leaves,
sharp as the taste of oak.
I pour, let the whiskey settle,
a quiet blaze in my glass.

Outside, the trees are bare —
a season stripped of its own skin,
standing, gaunt, in the cold.
I drink to them,
their loss, my own.

At Dusk, By the Fire

Fire snaps, its heat an old friend
on nights like this.
The whiskey bites, smooth as the fall,
warm as the thought of her voice —
just a thought, no more.

The glass grows lighter.
Her memory fades,
caught in the drift of wood smoke
against an early dark sky.

In the Quiet

The glass is amber against my hand,
fingers warm to the touch.
Outside, a chill fills the trees,
bare branches holding up the stars.
In here, the quiet stretches long.

I wonder if she ever stood like this,
whiskey in hand,
thinking about the end of things
while the autumn burned down outside.

Old Oak and Fire

There's a steadiness to it—
the weight of whiskey on the tongue,
the feel of its burn, slow, sure.

Outside, the wind picks up,
and a leaf scrapes across the window.
I drink to the sound,
the rough cut of wood and whiskey
in the fading light.

A Toast to the Night

It settles low, the taste of rye,
like the dusk that fills these rooms.
The fire's a quiet roar tonight,
keeping watch as the wind pulls
at the trees outside.

In the dark, I feel her there —
a shadow in the smoke,
a memory that never leaves.
Here's to her, to the night,
and the hollow sound
of an empty glass.

In Autumn's Shadow

The whiskey glows, a small sun
in a fading room.
Her name drifts up, unbidden,
caught in the amber light.
I let it rest, untouched.

Outside, the world's turning bare,
the wind a cold reminder.
Inside, I drink to its edge,
and the slow burn of forgetting.

Where Fire and Shadow Meet

The fire crackles low, casting amber light,
its warmth creeping like the slow burn of rye,
smooth but fierce, familiar yet strange.
Outside, the trees stand bare, stripped
by a season that knows only to take.
The whiskey's earthy, with hints of pine,
of the woodlands and of cold morning fog,
each sip a memory drawn from dark places.

I raise my glass to the silence, to the night,
to her name that hovers in the glow.
She was like this whiskey once — bold,
holding warmth like fire, bright in the glass,
then slipping away, just beyond reach.
I drink to forget, but she stays, a ghost in the glass,
her face lingering where the shadows dance.
I close my eyes, let the taste linger,
a sharpness softened by time but not by age.

In the quiet, I toast the wind outside,
howling like a wolf come to claim its due,
tearing through the dying leaves,
a reminder that no fire lasts forever.
The whiskey holds on, deep and steady,
as steady as I want to be, as steady as I fail to be,
caught between fire and shadow,
where memory clings like smoke in the air.

Under an Autumn Moon

The night is clear, sharp as glass,
and the moon hangs full over the trees,
its cold light pooling like whiskey's amber glow.
I pour another glass, feel the weight of it,
heavy as thoughts I can't shake,
filled with memories that slip in, silent as the stars.

She comes to me in these quiet moments,
in the bitterness that settles after each sip,
a taste that's not unwelcome,
yet cuts all the same. Her dark eyes flash,
a memory brought to life by the fire,
and I sit here, holding to warmth,
knowing she's just a shadow on the wall.

Leaves scatter outside, crimson and gold,
a last shout before they are lost,
and I feel that loss, deep as the burn
that whiskey leaves behind, warming and raw.
I drink to her, to the night, to things forgotten—
or nearly forgotten, for they return, always.

This season has its own kind of death,
leaves to the ground, nights to the cold,
and I sit here in the firelight's quiet roar,
watching it all pass by.
Her laugh, her voice, her touch—
it all lingers here, in the whiskey's haze,
a comfort, a curse, a taste that I'll chase
until the bottle runs dry.

The Familiar Sting

Amber glass in hand, I raise
A bitter warmth to swollen lips —
A soldier's drink, a lover's haze.
I sip, and somewhere memory slips.

Across the fire, embers burn,
Smoldering as they wait for ash;
In darkness, all things slowly turn,
With each smooth sip, the past falls back.

Once, a sky of gunpowder gray,
Now, only the still, worn shade
Of whisky's burn and slow decay —
In firelight's quiet, debts are paid.

The Last Watch

I've stood on midnight's ledge alone,
With whiskey braced against the cold,
Unmoved, as distant stars have shown
The long-forgotten tales they hold.

The moon, that silent soldier's eye,
Watches the night unfold in waves;
I drink, in kinship with the sky,
Each glass a prayer the darkness saves.

For those who went, and those who stayed —
All haunt the rim of every glass;
I drink for them, who never fade,
And feel them pass, and feel them pass.

Autumn's Quiet Burden

November's leaf falls brittle, still,
As memories like frost descend—
A burden borne against my will,
Of battles lost, and whispers penned.

The woods burn gold, and fading red,
And whisper of a world made whole;
Yet whiskey calls the quiet dead,
To warm my hand, to cool my soul.

In solitude, a soldier's peace,
When silence wraps me close in sound;
The fire snaps, the colors cease,
As autumn's leaves fold to the ground.

A Solitary Toast

I sit alone, my glass held high,
To absent friends and stories told;
To faces gone, but close nearby,
In amber depths, their glories bold.

With every sip, they settle near —
The fallen, quiet, unnamed few;
Each taste a letter, burnt but clear,
Their lives the words that whiskey knew.

The fire crackles soft and low,
Like voices heard in fading light;
I drink, they whisper as they go,
Lost shadows drifting into night.

The Glass and Autumn's Fire

When autumn's flame ignites the amber wood,
I raise a glass to shadows fading near,
In whiskey's warmth, I find what silence would —
A voice that calls through smoke, the lost made
clear.

The crackling fire whispers truths I know,
Of battles fought, in pastures far away;
Each sip recalls the chill, the ebb and flow,
Of soldiers' names that linger, yet decay.

Yet in this glass, they live and breathe once more,
As if the oak and earth could hold their face —
While autumn's leaves, like ashes from the war,
Descend in quiet peace, in solemn grace.

So to the flame, a final toast I make —
To memory's burn, to lives the whiskey wakes.

Leaves Fall with a Soldier's Burden

The leaves fall soft with a soldier's pain,
Amber tones drift down like a sigh,
Whiskey stirs, as memories wane —
Ghosts linger here, though quiet and shy.

Amber tones drift down like a sigh,
Their voices hidden in fire's glow.
Ghosts linger here, though quiet and shy,
Their faces blurred in the evening's flow.

Their voices hidden in fire's glow,
Fading slowly, yet never lost;
Their faces blurred in the evening's flow,
Bound to each sip, a soldier's cost.

Fading slowly, yet never lost,
Whiskey stirs, as memories wane,
Bound to each sip, a soldier's cost —
The leaves fall soft with a soldier's pain.

Unnamed

The leaves fell like ash—
orange and red embers scattered
by a wind sharp enough
to sting the skin.
The glass in my hand trembled,
amber liquid catching the dying sun.
A burn—smooth at first,
then raw, like an old wound.
Smoke curled from the cigar,
lazy and gray,
rising to a heaven
I no longer prayed to
Once, I knew the crackle of flames,
the shrill of alarms slicing the night,
the scent of scorched wood
and iron-rich blood.
Now, it's the hush I crave:
the weight of silence in autumn's air,
the kind that settles in the bones
and leaves you alone with yourself.
The whiskey does its work,
softening sharp edges,
fading faces that once looked to me—
for breath, for salvation.
But some ghosts linger.
They hang in the trees,
shadows dancing in fire-lit hues,
whispering my name with the wind.
So I pour another,
fingers steady now,
and watch the world die a little—

as it always does,
with grace,
and the promise of spring.

Ashes on the Breeze

The leaves spun down,
orange and red scraps of memory,
torn from branches too brittle
to hold on.
The whiskey sat warm in my palm,
its weight familiar,
like the heft of a helmet
or the pull of a hose
in the old days.
Smoke lingered in the air,
cigar tips glowing like the edges
of a distant fire
I no longer run toward.
There's a quiet now,
a heavy, aching kind —
thicker than the autumn air,
deeper than the scars
beneath my shirt.
Once, the sirens sang,
and I answered.
Flames kissed the night sky
while I tore breath from the jaws
of chaos. Now, the ghosts come slow,
like the breeze
that carries the scent of burning leaves.
They sit with me,
silent, in the fading gold of evening.
Another sip.
The whiskey burns like truth,
dulls like mercy.
I welcome both.

The Amber Flame

When autumn's burn ignites the amber wood,
I lift a glass where shadows flicker near.
In whiskey's warmth, the soul finds what it
would —
A fragile calm where voices reappear.
The crackling fire speaks of battles waged,
Of nights when fear and fire lit the skies.
Each sip stirs winds of fields where war once
raged,
And faces rise, though time and ash disguise.
A soldier's cry, a comrade's final breath —
The oak and earth now bear their weight and
name.
The leaves descend like whispers of their death,
Soft echoes tied to autumn's fleeting flame.
To fire, a toast — to shadows left behind,
To fleeting warmth where loss and peace align.

The Soldier's Autumn

The leaves fall soft, a soldier's weary ache,
With whispered tones that drift through autumn's
glow.
Whiskey stirs as memories wake —
Ghosts rise where shadows weave the fire's slow
flow.
With whispered tones that drift through autumn's
glow,
Their voices echo in the cooling breeze.
Ghosts rise where shadows weave the fire's slow
flow,
Faces fleeting, caught between the trees.
Their voices echo in the cooling breeze,
Fading sharp, like glass against the light.
Faces fleeting, caught between the trees,
Bound to each sip, each echo of the fight.
Fading sharp, like glass against the light,
Whiskey stirs as memories wake —
Bound to each sip, each hollowed night,
The leaves fall soft, a soldier's ache.

Autumn Wind

The amber sits heavy in the glass,
like a memory you never quite forget—
sipped slow, on the edge of dusk.
Autumn winds waltz through the windows,
rattling the branches—
those same trees,
year after year, their leaves dying
as I drink away the ghosts.
I hear them still, their voices slipping
between the ash and smoke,
hovering in the air like whispers from
war's long arms.
The fire crackles—its warmth a gentle lie,
offering fleeting comfort,the kind that fades
when the world's chill seeps back in.
In the quiet, I think of the men
who stayed behind,
their faces flickering
in the firelight.
The ones I left with no goodbyes,
no time for closure.
I drink to them—to the ghosts I've met
and those I'll never know.
Each sip, a heavy toast
to memory, to regret.
And still, the fire burns on,
its soft glow turning the past
just a shade lighter, before the darkness
settles again.

Whiskey's Breath

The air smells different now, like cigars and
autumn—
a sharp, biting scent that wraps around me,
tight as the past, pulling me closer
to its jagged edge.
I let the wind take the ash, let the smoke
curl upward, fading like the days
I can't remember but feel in my bones,
etched there like shadows of a life
I keep trying to leave behind.
The fire burns low, its glow flickering—
a soft, uneven pulse, like the soldiers' faces
that come to me in the night,
or the voices from streets in foreign lands
where I never truly belonged.
But there's joy in this, too.
The feel of wind weaving through the trees,
its weight pressing against my chest—
a silent command to breathe,
to hold onto this moment and remember
the man I was before the battles
and the man I am now,
standing steady beneath the autumn sky.
The air clears slowly,
whiskey dulls the ache for another night,
and for a moment, I am just a man,
watching the world shift with the season—
autumn slipping gently through the door
as the earth settles into quiet once more.

Autumn Whiskey

The whiskey burns slow as it slips down, warming his throat like an old memory, bittersweet and lingering. The fire crackles in the hearth, throwing long, restless shadows that flicker against the walls like ghosts of the past. Smoke from his cigar spirals upward, mingling with the scent of burning oak—an aroma he's come to associate with these solitary autumn nights.
He's middle-aged now, worn by the steady erosion of time, the years slipping by unnoticed like leaves tumbling in the wind. Outside, the trees whisper to the breeze, their voices soft and mournful, carrying the chill of the season. He listens, and it feels like a voice he once knew—a voice steeped in loss, murmuring of his father, long gone. In the dim glow of the fire, the memory of his father flickers faintly, no longer solid, no longer loud. Once, this room had been alive with laughter, the air thick with joy and presence. Now it holds only silence, broken by the occasional sigh of the wind or the creak of settling wood.
He watches the flames dance, their light casting echoes of the past: younger days when the air was free of regret, when life held a clean simplicity and the promise of a tomorrow untainted by loss. But that was before. Before the years weighed heavy on his shoulders, before death hollowed out spaces in his life that could never be filled again. The whiskey in his glass dwindles, the cigar burns low, leaving behind a faint haze of smoke and a familiar ache that settles deep in his chest.

Outside, the wind whispers once more, carrying with it the names of things lost, the fragments of a life he cannot reclaim.

He lets the quiet take over, lets it seep into his bones as it always does in autumn. The wind, steady and eternal, moves through the trees, through the room, through him—speaking not just of time passing, but of what remains. And for a fleeting moment, he is simply a man in the soft glow of firelight, watching the world grow still.

The River's Quiet Grace

The sun dips low and casts its golden glow,
Its light ignites the fields in fiery hue.
The breeze begins to stir, a gentle flow,
And draws the eye toward where the river grew.
It cuts the land, a vein both deep and wise,
Its waters soft, yet ever-moving, strong.
A hawk ascends beneath the twilight skies,
Its shadow trailing as it glides along.
The river whispers secrets as it slides,
A ceaseless rhythm, ancient, unafraid.
Its current claims the leaf that fate decides,
A fleeting moment in the dance it made.
In quiet grace, the earth lets time erase,
Yet beauty lingers in its still embrace.

The Last Cigarette

The night was cold, the air thin with smoke.
A faded neon sign buzzed, its dim glow barely cutting
Through the fogged-up windows. He sat alone,
Elbows planted on the table, hands curled tight
Around an old glass, whiskey swirling like ghosts
Of roads long traveled. His boots, worn smooth
By years of wandering, rested heavy on the floor,
Anchoring a man who had seen too much.
There was a woman once — Lily, her name.
She had flowers in her hair and eyes
That sparkled like the river in spring.
But she was gone, like summer's fleeting warmth,
Leaving him with a memory too vivid to fade.
He wondered if she ever thought of him,
In a world that spun on without his shadow.
He didn't know if she was still alive,
But the velvet softness of her lips lingered,
A phantom, like the smell of cigarettes
That clung to his jacket long after the pack was gone.
His hand found the last cigarette.
He lit it, the flame kissing its tip,
And in the tiny ember, her face appeared again —
Young, laughing, full of hope.
He inhaled deeply, the burn sharp in his chest,
And exhaled slowly, like releasing a burden
He'd carried far too long. The bar door creaked open.
The wind surged in, tangling with faint sirens in the distance.

A man walked past, trailing the scent of rain.
The cigarette burned down to its stub,
And he crushed it into the ashtray.
The ashes, like pieces of a life once lived,
Were left behind, Scattered, forgotten, and still.

Whiskey and Autumn Winds

Whiskey settles slow,
Dark and smooth,
Clinging to my throat
Like the last words left unsaid.
Outside, the autumn wind
Whispers through restless trees,
Tugging at the threads of time.
And I,
A man weathered by years and loss,
Sip slowly,
Letting the fire in my chest burn quiet.
The leaves drift down,
Soft as fading memories,
Their fall mirroring
Words that never found form.
In the stillness of the room,
Laughter echoes faintly,
A love dissolving like smoke.
The fire crackles,
Its warmth steady but fleeting.
I reach for the bottle again —
Not to escape,
But for the comfort of something familiar,
Something that feels like home.
For a moment, it lingers.
Then, the wind whispers goodbye.

A Slow Burn in the Autumn Light

The whiskey swirled, amber flames in the glass,
A slow burn that kissed the tongue, bittersweet.
The air outside carried leaves that amass,
Their final waltz a crumbling, golden fleet.
By the hearth, shadows danced, long and thin,
A memory stirred in the curling smoke.
The oak of the bottle, the warmth within,
Kindled her voice in the words she once spoke.
Her dark eyes haunted like a raven's call,
Soft, persistent, as the fire's glow waned.
Each sip unraveled the threads of it all,
Yet her essence in the whiskey remained.
Autumn sighed through the panes, cool and
aware,
Bearing the weight of love that lingers there.

Bourbon's Confession

The bourbon whispered truths beneath its breath,
As frost crept upon the trembling windowpane.
It tasted of solace, a life after death,
Of seasons fading but never in vain.
The woodsmoke curled like secrets in the air,
Its fingers tracing paths unseen, untold.
And there, in the ember's despairing glare,
Lay dreams of warmth that were once bright and
bold.
Each sip was a hymn to the fleeting days,
A dance of maple and hemlock, entwined.
Her laughter echoed through this autumn haze,
A phantom melody love left behind.
Still, the whiskey consoled the broken man,
In every drop, a life's attempt began.
Would you like more in this style or with
additional themes woven in?

Amber Harvest

The glass in hand reflects the dying light,
A golden hue that whispers to the tongue.
It tastes of harvest, fields kissed by the night,
Of stories told and autumn songs unsung.
The whiskey hums of cinnamon and smoke,
Its warmth a hearth that battles evening's chill.
The maple lingers, sweet as words once spoke,
Yet bitter, like the leaves upon the hill.
The forest looms, its limbs a russet maze,
The crunch of earth a hymn to seasons past.
Each sip invokes those softer, ambered days,
As fleeting as the shadows autumn casts.
The fire crackles; in its glowing hue,
A thousand dreams rise up and fade from view.

A Pantoum of Maple and Fire

The whiskey whispers secrets to the air,
Its amber light reflects the forest's glow.
The hearth ignites the comfort found in care,
While autumn's breath is brisk, the leaves let go.
Its amber light reflects the forest's glow,
The glass is warm, the flavor sweet with pine.
While autumn's breath is brisk, the leaves let go,
Each sip a memory of love, divine.
The glass is warm, the flavor sweet with pine,
The cigar's smoke curls slowly toward the sky.
Each sip a memory of love, divine,
Yet bitter notes of longing still apply.
The cigar's smoke curls slowly toward the sky,
The whiskey whispers secrets to the air.
Yet bitter notes of longing still apply,
The hearth ignites the comfort found in care.

Melancholy of the Flame

The flame called softly from its cedar bed,
A crackling voice that soothed the autumn air.
It sang of fields where summer once had fled,
And warmed the shadows lurking on the stair.
The whiskey watched, its amber glow alive,
It swirled, recalling harvest moons long past.
The taste of maple lingered, sweet, contrived,
While cinnamon danced bold, yet could not last.
The forest whispered truths it could not keep,
Its leaves, like fleeting dreams, began to fall.
The man, alone, sat drinking autumn's deep,
His thoughts a fire that memory would stall.
And in the glass, her face began to gleam,
A phantom born of whiskey's amber stream.

The Forest Speaks in Amber Hues

The forest speaks in hues of red and gold,
Its branches heavy with the weight of time.
The bourbon glows, its warmth a tale retold,
Of autumn's fleeting beauty, near sublime.
It tastes of bark, of pine, of brittle leaves,
A liquid fire born of nature's core.
It whispers comfort as the evening weaves
A shroud of twilight—memories restore.
The man sits silent, wrapped in autumn's glow,
His cigar a plume of stories left unsaid.
The whiskey laughs, its tones a soft, deep woe,
As nature folds her quilt of orange and red.
The hearth provides, yet isolation binds,
For in the glass, he seeks what he can't find.
Would you like additional pieces or adjustments
to these?

Cinnamon Winds

The cinnamon winds play tricks upon the air,
They swirl through branches, stealing autumn's
gold.
Their scent ignites a memory laid bare,
Of bourbon nights and stories once retold.
The glass, half-empty, holds a fleeting sun,
Its warmth a tether to the dying day.
The amber tide, a river come undone,
Runs slow but steady, washing grief away.
The leaves descend like whispers from the sky,
Their voices hushed, yet still they seem to speak.
Each falling shape, a fragment of goodbye,
A fleeting solace for the lost and weak.
And still, the whiskey burns, its spice alive,
A bitter proof that memories survive.

A Pantoum of Hearth and Smoke

The fire dances in its auburn glow,
Its breath of cedar thick upon the air.
The whiskey sighs, its amber smooth and slow,
While solitude envelops in its care.
Its breath of cedar thick upon the air,
The cigar curls a ribbon into night.
While solitude envelops in its care,
The autumn forest fades from burning sight.
The cigar curls a ribbon into night,
The flavors blend—a warmth, a fleeting fire.
The autumn forest fades from burning sight,
Yet lingers in the shadows of desire.
The flavors blend—a warmth, a fleeting fire,
The fire dances in its auburn glow.
Yet lingers in the shadows of desire,
The whiskey sighs, its amber smooth and slow.

Maple's Melancholy

The maple bends to autumn's sharp decree,
Its leaves, like embers, drift to meet the ground.
A carpet woven soft, in red's esprit,
Each thread a symbol lost and newly found.
The bourbon murmurs of the forest deep,
Of roots entwined in earth's eternal hold.
Its taste, a story autumn longs to keep,
Of oaks that sway beneath the harvest's gold.
The man reclines, a figure carved in stone,
His thoughts, as aged as barrels filled with fire.
The flavors bloom, yet leave him there alone,
A fleeting spark to fuel his lost desire.
For every sip revives her shadowed face,
A memory no whiskey can erase.

The Last Ember

The last ember sighed beneath the grate,
Its dying breath a mournful ode to fall.
The man, glass poised, considered fleeting fate,
And how the seasons come to claim us all.
The whiskey laughed — its maple bite alive,
Its tones of honey sharp against the tongue.
Yet in its mirth, her memory would thrive,
A song of longing every sip had sung.
The forest framed the scene, its leaves alight,
Their colors bold against the somber gray.
Each branch extended fingers toward the night,
As though to keep the fading warmth at bay.
The fire dimmed, the room grew quiet, still,
And in the silence, whiskey broke his will.

Echoes of Harvest

The air is ripe with the scent of fallen fruit,
Apples crushed underfoot release their cry.
A golden harvest whispers at its root,
Yet shadows loom as twilight claims the sky.
A glass of bourbon waits, its amber deep,
Reflecting firelight's soft, unsteady gleam.
Its warmth stirs echoes buried in their sleep,
A memory rising like an autumn dream.
Her laughter lingers in the cinnamon breeze,
A phantom tune that dances through the trees.
The forest holds its breath, a quiet plea,
To freeze the hour, to let her spirit be.
Yet time is cruel, it takes and never mends,
The harvest fades, as every season ends.

Smoldering Leaves

The smoke of leaves, a hymn to days long past,
It lingers sweet upon the autumn air.
A whiskey glass reflects the fire's last,
Its glow a fragile promise, burning bare.
It lingers sweet upon the autumn air,
A fleeting warmth that neither fades nor stays.
Its glow a fragile promise, burning bare,
A hint of amber light through misty haze.
A fleeting warmth that neither fades nor stays,
The fire stirs its coals, a restless heart.
A hint of amber light through misty haze,
A taste of longing only flames impart.
The fire stirs its coals, a restless heart,
The smoke of leaves, a hymn to days long past.
A taste of longing only flames impart,
A whiskey glass reflects the fire's last.

A Song of Cask and Flame

The cask held stories bound in oak and grain,
Its seal unbroken until autumn's plea.
A toast was raised to both delight and pain,
To all the fleeting beauty we can see.
He drank to her, his lips still formed her name,
Though years had passed since last her shadow
fell.
The whiskey burned, but never matched the flame
Of dark-brown eyes that cast their secret spell.
The fire roared, as if to drown regret,
Yet in its chaos lay a quiet ache.
A fleeting solace born of fire met,
A whispered truth the amber dared to make.
The drink, the leaves, the smoke — they all
conspire,
To hold the heart within autumn's burning pyre.

The Forest Keeps Its Watch

The forest guards its treasures close at hand,
Each leaf a relic kissed by fleeting time.
Its amber hues, a painter's fleeting stand,
Transform the earth into a work sublime.
Beneath its boughs, the whiskey warms the soul,
Its heat a rival to the hearth inside.
A gentle burn that makes the spirit whole,
A steady friend when memories collide.
He sits alone, his glass a fragile truth,
A fragile echo of a love once known.
The autumn whispers, patient with its proof,
That nature takes but also makes its own.
For though the world may shift and leaves will
fall,
The whiskey's warmth remains, a cure for all.

The Barrel's Lament

In darkness, I waited,
oak and char my only companions.
Amber rivers ran through my veins,
whispering secrets of fire and patience.
Time sang to me,
its melody slow and deliberate,
each note carving wisdom into my wooden walls.
Autumn leaves fell outside,
their colors unknown to me,
yet their scent lingered in the sap of my soul.
When I opened,
I poured out memory, not liquid.
Each drop an elegy for the hands that held me,
the lips that kissed me,
the souls that sought solace within my amber
heart.

An Autumn Whisper, a Lover's Voice

The wind carries her voice through the trees,
a delicate hum, soft as the dying light.
It caresses the amber liquid in his glass,
sending ripples through his reflection.
Each sip is a meeting —
her dark eyes swim in the warmth of maple and
smoke.
The cinnamon burn on his tongue
mimics her laugh, sharp but fleeting,
and he swallows her absence whole.
The trees shed their skins like old regrets,
but he holds fast to his,
wrapped tight in memories
that the whiskey only deepens.
The fire crackles; it speaks for him.
He lets it.

The Alchemy of Autumn

In the alchemy of autumn,
leaves burn gold without the touch of flame.
The forest transforms,
a crucible of amber, rust, and ruby hues.
The whiskey, too, is an alchemist —
turning oak to warmth, grain to comfort.
Each glass mirrors the season's transformation,
its amber depths alive with the fire of creation.
And yet, he sits still,
a statue carved from solitude,
watching the world turn to beauty,
only to fall apart.
The fireplace breathes life into the silence,
its smoke curling like an unanswered question.
He raises his glass,
not in toast,
but in surrender.

A Conversation with the Hearth

The fire is a friend tonight,
its crackle an answer to questions
he dares not ask aloud.
"Do you remember her?" he whispers,
and the flames nod, casting her shadow
on the wooden walls.
The whiskey is silent but knowing.
It cradles his despair,
its weight both heavy and light,
its burn a paradox of pain and comfort.
Outside, the wind gathers leaves like memories,
only to scatter them again.
He drinks deeply,
as if to fill the void with amber truths,
but the glass lies empty.
The hearth sighs. So does he.

The Color of Longing

What color is longing?
He thinks it must be amber,
like the whiskey in his glass,
or the light that filters through autumn leaves.
It tastes of maple and smoke,
with a hint of regret that clings to the tongue.
It smells of earth after rain,
rich and loamy,
and the faint spice of burning wood.
Longing feels like a chill that the fire can't reach,
a weight that the drink can't lift.
It sounds like the rustle of leaves in an empty
forest,
the quiet sigh of a season's end.
Longing is amber,
and it lives within him.

The Amber Mirror

The glass in his hand is no longer whiskey —
it is a mirror, liquid and knowing.
It reflects not his face but his years,
filtered through oak and shadow.
The amber depths hold his choices,
each sip a chapter of lives unlived,
roads untaken.
The burn on his tongue whispers truths
he would rather forget,
yet the flavor lingers, demanding he listen.
Outside, the trees surrender their leaves to the
wind, a quiet resignation he envies.
He swirls the glass,
watching the liquid trace circles of what could
have been.
In the end, he drinks it anyway.

Harvest of the Soul

Autumn is a reckoning,
a harvest not of grain, but of time.
The amber fields glow with a fleeting fire,
each stalk bending to the weight of inevitability.

The whiskey echoes the season,
a distillation of longing and light.
Its warmth wraps him like the hearth's embrace,
but its taste is heavy with the knowledge
that all fires must fade.

He wonders if the trees feel their own endings,
if they hear the whisper of decay in their roots.
He raises his glass,
toasts the dying leaves,
and drinks to their courage.

The Stillness of Smoke

Cigar smoke curls toward the ceiling,
its lazy ascent a study in freedom.
He watches it dissolve,
a metaphor too perfect to ignore.
The whiskey rests in his hand,
its amber glow a small sun,
a reminder of warmth in the vast chill of his
thoughts.
"Why does it matter?" he asks the fire.
The flames answer in crackles and sparks,
language he cannot decode
but feels all the same.
Outside, the wind scatters the leaves,
their dance both beautiful and futile.
He drinks deeply,
as if to capture that same fleeting grace.

An Autumn Paradox

Autumn holds two truths in its hands—
the abundance of harvest
and the emptiness of falling leaves.
The forest wears its colors boldly,
even as it prepares to shed them.
The whiskey mirrors this paradox:
its warmth is fleeting,
its burn eternal.
Each sip is a reminder
that joy and sorrow are not opposites,
but companions.
He sits alone,
his thoughts as tangled as the branches outside.
The fire burns low,
its light barely reaching his face,
but he feels its heat
and wonders if that is enough.

The Amber Philosopher

The bottle is a philosopher,
its truths poured in amber riddles.
It asks him questions
he cannot answer sober —
questions about love,
about loss,
about the meaning of the autumn leaves.
Each sip is an argument
between fire and sweetness,
a debate that leaves him silent.
The fireplace crackles its approval,
its heat an ally in the cold war of his thoughts.
The forest outside watches,
its bare branches pointing skyward
as if seeking absolution.
He does not pray.
He only drinks.

The Hearth's Shadow

The fire casts shadows on the wall,
dancing figures of light and absence.
He watches them,
their movements a language older than words.
The whiskey speaks in softer tones,
its warmth a whisper against the chill of the room.
He listens,
not to the fire,
but to the spaces between its crackles —
the silence that carries her voice.
Autumn waits outside,
its breath fogging the windowpanes.
He waits inside,
his breath carrying the weight of unsaid things.
The shadows fade as the fire dies,
but the whiskey lingers,
a ghost in his glass.

Amber Horizons

Whiskey lingers, amber deep,
A quiet song before I sleep.
The leaves, ablaze, fall one by one,
Their fleeting dance beneath the sun.
Each sip a tale, both sharp and sweet,
A forest path beneath my feet.
The burn reminds of life undone,
Of fleeting moments, battles won.
The trees bow low to autumn's breath,
Their beauty tied to coming death.
And in my glass, the seasons blend—
A beginning born within an end.

Echoes in the Glass

In the amber's glow, I see her face,
A fleeting ghost, a vanished grace.
Dark hair framed by autumn's fire,
A memory etched, a lost desire.
Each sip calls forth her soft brown eyes,
A forest rich, where silence lies.
The whiskey whispers truths I fear,
Of times now gone, yet still so near.
The glass, a mirror to the soul,
Shows cracks where love has left its toll.
And though I drink to drown the ache,
Her shadow lingers in its wake.

Cinders and Smoke *(Pantoum)*

The fireplace hums a quiet tune,
Its embers glow like fading years.
Whiskey warms beneath the moon,
Yet autumn brings its share of tears.
Its embers glow like fading years,
The forest whispers tales of old.
Yet autumn brings its share of tears,
A fleeting warmth against the cold.
The forest whispers tales of old,
As whiskey dulls the bitter sting.
A fleeting warmth against the cold,
The hearth my solace, bourbon king.
As whiskey dulls the bitter sting,
The fireplace hums a quiet tune.
The hearth my solace, bourbon king—
Whiskey warms beneath the moon.

Beneath the Maple Canopy

Beneath the maple's crimson crown,
I sit with whiskey, staring down.
The glass reflects the forest's glow,
Where autumn whispers truths we know.
The sweet of maple warms my throat,
Its notes like stories poets wrote.
Each sip a bridge to seasons past,
A fleeting joy, too bright to last.
I watch the leaves drift soft and slow,
Their fate is mine; we both must go.
Yet in this amber, life remains—
A fleeting spark through autumn's veins.

Silent Companion

In the quiet, whiskey waits,
Its warmth like fire, sealing fates.
The glass, a friend through autumn's chill,
Speaks softly now, but always will.

Autumn's Offering

The forest yields its final gift,
A golden sea where branches lift.
Their leaves, like whiskey, rich and rare,
Float softly through the crisp, cool air.
The oak bows low, the maple bends,
As autumn signals summer's end.
The glass reflects the fleeting hues,
Of skies aflame in sunset's muse.
I drink to toast what cannot last,
To fleeting futures, dying pasts.
For every autumn's bittersweet,
Reminds the soul its time is fleet.

Bourbon and Ashes

The fire dies, its embers fade,
A fleeting warmth the hearth has made.
Whiskey in hand, I watch the glow,
A mirror to the life I know.

Harvest of Memory

Upon the field where summer's warmth has fled,
The harvest whispers, bound by autumn's hand.
The leaves descend, like whispers for the dead,
While whiskey flows, a warmth the cold demands.
Its burn is sharp, a fire to the chest,
A fleeting flame that echoes in my veins.
I think of days when youth burned bright,
unrest—
Before the frost of time had claimed its gains.
Yet here I sit, with glass and fire's glow,
Reflecting on the years both bright and grim.
The earth will take me back, this much I know,
But for tonight, I sip life to the brim.

Crimson Shadows

The forest sings in autumn's key,
A mournful tune of what must be.
The leaves fall gently, kissed by flame,
Each one a soul, no two the same.
Bourbon warms, its amber bright,
A fire contained, defying night.
Its taste, a map of earth and wood,
Of fleeting joys misunderstood.
I drink, alone, in twilight's glow,
While autumn winds begin to blow.
The trees stand bare, their strength laid plain,
A lesson carved from joy and pain.
This season speaks of things undone,
Of fading light, of setting sun.
And though the whiskey soothes my frame,
Its burn reminds we end the same.

A Fireside Elegy

The bottle sits with time-worn grace,
Its amber depths a fleeting trace.
A mirror to the autumn's breath,
Where beauty walks the edge of death.
The glass is raised to skies aflame,
To fleeting joys that have no name.
The air is sharp, the earth laid bare,
A quiet ache hangs everywhere.
Each sip ignites the soul's refrain,
A melody of joy and pain.
The burn endures, untamed, unbound,
The warmth, a solace gently found.
Here's to the leaves that kiss the ground,
To whiskey's truths, both lost and found.
For life's a fire that ebbs and glows,
A fleeting warmth the spirit knows.

Fleeting Flight

The maple whispers, burning bright,
Its leaves adrift in fleeting flight.
Like embers cast from nature's pyre,
They flicker out, their brief desire.
Whiskey glows, a golden hue,
Its warmth a fire both old and new.
A velvet sting, a tender burn,
It speaks of seasons as they turn.
Within its depths, the earth takes hold,
A fleeting tale in liquid gold.
And as the glass runs smooth and low,
The autumn fades in twilight's glow.
Yet in this moment, still and pure,
Life finds its flame, its fleeting cure.

Where Autumn Ends

Here, where the fire burns low
and the whiskey sits untouched,
autumn folds itself into quiet.
The leaves have fallen,
scattered like pages of a story untold.
The forest, once alive in amber and crimson,
is now a silhouette —
a memory etched against the gray sky.
He exhales slowly,
his breath mingling with the last of the cigar's
smoke,
a final offering to the room.
Here, surrounded by wood and flame,
he is no longer haunted by her face
nor the ache of years untamed.
The whiskey whispers its farewell,
its warmth lingering as it always does.
He stands, feeling the weight of endings,
and steps into the night,
where the first frost glitters on the ground,
and the wind carries the scent of smoke and pine.
It is here, where autumn ends,
that he begins again.

The Last Pour

The bottle is nearly empty,
a glass's worth of time left to swallow.
It sits on the table,
bathed in the fire's dim glow,
a relic of nights that held more answers than
questions.
The forest outside is quiet now,
its winds no longer howling their discontent.
Even the trees have settled into their bareness,
resigned to the truth of the season.
He pours slowly, reverently —
the last amber drop falling like a final word.
In the glass, he sees the harvest of his thoughts:
regret and peace,
longing and release.
The whiskey burns as it goes down,
a small fire against the dying embers.
When the glass is empty,
he sets it beside the bottle
and watches the flames disappear
into nothing but smoke.

Epilogue

The legacy of Ernest Hemingway is one of profound complexity, weaving through the corridors of literary brilliance and the shadows of personal struggle. Hemingway's life was marked by a relentless pursuit of authenticity, both in his writing and his experiences. From his tenure as an ambulance driver in World War I, where he confronted the raw, unfiltered realities of human suffering, to his relentless battle with his own inner demons, Hemingway's journey resonates deeply with my own.

As an EMT on an ambulance, I have walked a parallel path, bearing witness to the fragility of life and the stark realities of pain and loss. The sirens that pierce the night, the hurried footsteps to the scene of an emergency, and the countless lives held in the balance are echoes of Hemingway's wartime experiences. His ambulance driving in the trenches of WWI and my own rides through the urban landscape are bound by a shared thread of confronting mortality and the relentless quest to make sense of it all.

Hemingway's literary works are imbued with a raw, unvarnished truth, capturing the essence of the human condition with a simplicity that belies its depth. His struggles with mental health, exacerbated by the harrowing experiences of war and his own personal battles, mirror my own challenges as a poet and EMT. The weight of each emergency call, the faces of those I could not save, and the emotional toll of constant exposure to trauma have often driven me to the brink of despair and madness.

Yet, like Hemingway, I have found solace and meaning in the written word. Poetry has become my refuge, a way to process the chaos and find clarity amidst the turmoil. The imagery of autumn leaves, the warmth of whiskey, and the introspective calm of nature serve as metaphors for the healing process. Through my verses, I attempt to navigate the darkness, shedding light on the shadows that linger within.

Hemingway's life was a testament to the delicate balance between creative genius and personal torment. His ability to capture the beauty and brutality of life with such vivid clarity has inspired my own poetic journey. In facing my mental health challenges, I draw strength from his resilience, finding my voice amidst the cacophony of emergency sirens and the silence of introspection.

As we close this collection, I reflect on the parallels between our lives. Hemingway's struggle to find meaning and peace in a world scarred by conflict and suffering is a journey I know all too well. His words, much like my own, are a testament to the enduring power of art to heal, to illuminate, and to connect us to the deeper truths of our existence.

In honoring Hemingway's legacy and sharing my own story, I hope to bridge the gap between past and present, offering a beacon of hope to those who face similar battles. Through the lens of poetry, may we find the strength to confront our demons and the grace to embrace the light that lies beyond.

With heartfelt gratitude, I wish you all the best.

Hemingway's Whiskey

It sits in the glass, a still resolve,
A burn that whispers, a riddle to solve.
The amber glints, like the fading sun,
A battle fought, yet never won.

The taste is rough, like salt and sea,
A sailor's tale of agony.
It tells of wounds both deep and wide,
Of truths we drink but cannot hide.

Each sip is a bullet, clean and sharp,
A note of despair, a mournful harp.
It stings the tongue, then soothes the throat,
A paradox in every note.

It's the call of the wild, the pull of the fight,
The lonely vigils in the night.
It's the pain of love, the weight of loss,
The bitter end, the final cost.

In Hemingway's whiskey, a life laid bare —
A toast to courage, to wounds we wear.
For in its depths, we see our face,
A fleeting shadow, a human trace.